Legends of Rock & Roll

Simon & Garfunkel

An unauthorized fan tribute

By: James Hoag

"Legends of Rock & Roll – Simon & Garfunkel" Copyright 2014 James Hoag. All rights reserved. Manufactured in the United States of America. No parts of this book may be reproduced in any form or by any electronic or mechanical means including information storage and retrieval systems without written permission from the publisher. The only exception is for a reviewer. A reviewer may quote brief passages in a review. Published by www.number1project.com Monument Marketing Publishing LTD., 53 Hanover Dr., Orem, Utah 84058

Paperback Edition

Other Paperbacks by James Hoag

Legends of Rock and Roll Series

Legends of Rock & Roll Volume 1 - The Fifties

Legends of Rock & Roll Volume 2 - The Sixties

Legends of Rock & Roll Volume 3 - The Seventies

The Beatles

Queen

Individual Beatles

John Lennon

Paul McCartney

George Harrison

Ringo Starr

Fifties

Everly Brothers

Sixties

Neil Diamond

Roy Orbison

The Beach Boys

Bob Dylan

The Doors

The Bee Gees

The Grateful Dead

Seventies

Eagles

Bruce Springsteen

Eighties

Madonna

Legends of Country Music

Reba McEntire

Willie Nelson

Johnny Cash

George Jones

Merle Haggard

Garth Brooks

Waylon Jennings

(All Available at Amazon.com)

James Hoag

Table of Contents

Introduction	9
The Early Years	10
Tom and Jerry	14
Taking a Break from Music	18
Signing on with Columbia	22
"The Sound of Silence"	24
Then Lightning Struck	28
"Parsley, Sage, Rosemary, and Thyme"	32
The Drug Years	35
"Mrs. Robinson"	37
"Catch-22"	40
"The Boxer"	42
Female Companionship	44
"Bridge Over Troubled Water"	47
Paul Simon Alone	51
Art Garfunkel Alone	54
"There Goes Rhymin' Simon"	56

Problems At Home	58
"My Little Town"	60
"Annie Hall"	62
Carrie Fisher	64
The Central Park Concert	66
"Graceland"	70
In the Years Since	72
Legacy of Simon & Garfunkel	74
Afterword	76
About the Author	78
Selected Discography	79

James Hoag

INTRODUCTION

If you've read my very first *Legends of Rock & Roll* book about the Everly Brothers, then you might remember that in 2005, my wife and I attended the reunion concert of Simon & Garfunkel. The Everlys played during the intermission of the show, but the rest of the show was all Paul Simon and Art Garfunkel.

Now, Paul and Art were not young guys. Both men were in their early sixties when we saw them, but you would never know it. The harmonies were still there. The songs sounded the same. The audience sang along with them. This was the music of a generation; the music of the Sixties.

It was a magical night. I had never heard the guys perform live, and they performed all of their hits, as well as a lot of the solo work which they had recorded over the years. My wife and I came away singing all of the songs.

I have always liked Simon & Garfunkel, even before they were Simon & Garfunkel. I remember Tom & Jerry from the late Fifties. I didn't know at the time (no one did) what they would become, but I knew I liked the sound and the songs, but Tom & Jerry didn't find a place in our history; it took a name change and a change of sound to accomplish that. They were destined to become one of the most famous duos in music history: Simon & Garfunkel.

THE EARLY YEARS

I flipped a coin and Paul won so let's deal with him first. Paul was born Paul Frederic Simon on October 13, 1941 in Newark, New Jersey. His father was Louis Simon and his mother's name was Belle. Paul came by his musical ability honestly as his father was a bass player for a band which played on the radio. Mom was an elementary school teacher. Paul had one younger brother, Eddie, who was born in 1945 and Eddie turned out to be musically inclined as well, but, of course, wasn't the success that Paul later became.

Even though Paul was born in Newark, the family soon moved to Kew Gardens near Forest Hills, New York which is a suburb of Queens. This was a nice middle-class neighborhood, and Paul grew up in a loving and fairly normal family. At that time, Paul had no idea that just three blocks away and just three weeks after Paul was born, a baby came to the Garfunkel family that they named Artie.

Art was born Arthur Ira Garfunkel on November 5, 1941, just three weeks after Paul. Art's parents were Jack and Rose Garfunkel. Jack was a travelling salesman. He marketed his own products which he had invented and, as far as I can tell, did very well at it. Mom was a secretary. He had two brothers. His older brother, Jules, was three years older than Art, and his younger brother, Jerome, was four years younger than Art, so Art was a middle child. I can't find any evidence that it affected him much one way or another.

You can't talk about either of the boys without mentioning the other one. They were both Jewish and knew of each other from the first grade on. Paul came from a musical family as his dad played with a band, but Art had no such upbringing. He got his start just listening to the radio. From as early an age as he can remember, he would sing along with the radio and it was soon discovered that Art had perfect pitch. He would sing almost everywhere he went, and he really didn't care who heard him.

By first grade Art and Paul were in the same class at PS 164 in Queens. However, they really weren't friends at this point. They, of course, knew of each other's existence but no spark of friendship had occurred, yet. Paul first became aware of Art's talent in the third grade when the school put on a talent show and Art sang the old Nat King Cole song "Too Young." You might remember the song: "They tried to tell us we were too young." It's a beautiful song and was a number one hit for Cole in 1951. Art was nine years old, and the girls loved it.

Suddenly, Paul saw that music could be a way to a girl's heart. I'm not sure I was thinking about girls at age nine, but Paul was. Paul knew he wanted to work in music but hadn't quite settled on a direction. However, at age ten, his father happened to pass by his room when Paul was practicing singing. Dad was dressed in a tuxedo, getting ready to go out for a gig with his band, and he stopped and said to Paul, "That's nice, Paul, real nice." Paul was blown away. He knew that if his father believed in him, he could do almost anything. I think it was at that moment that Paul knew that music was what he wanted to do with his life. I am amazed by this story because not all parents are as supportive of their children as Louis Simon was. In one off-handed remark, he solidified Paul's future.

The singing that Paul was doing when his dad happened by was from a stage production of *Alice in Wonderland* that the school was doing. Paul had the part of the White Rabbit in the production, and Art played the Cheshire Cat. It was during rehearsal for this school play that the boys finally got close enough to realize that they could be real friends. They were both loners and really not part of the school social scene. They discovered they liked the same things and were both planning similar futures. Why not work together?

They were eleven years old.

Even though both boys were Jewish, Art came from a much more traditional family than Paul did. Paul said his father really didn't believe in religion but his mother did and went to synagogue about once a year. Art, on the other hand, faced what all Jewish boys face when they turn thirteen: Bar Mitzvah. It impressed me that Art served as the cantor at his own Bar Mitzvah.

In 1954, rock and roll was just starting to be heard in the United States. New York City was the heart of the new sound and many of the singers would go on to become legends in that genre. Since Paul and Art lived in New York and were growing up there, they got a sneak peek at the future when Alan Freed came to town with his show which he called *Rock and Roll Party*. Freed had become popular as a disc jockey in Cleveland, Ohio, but wanted a bigger audience than Cleveland could provide, so he brought his radio show to New York. Naturally, Paul and Art both heard the show, and they were hooked on the music. They would both stay up late at night and listen to the show which broadcast on WINS each night from seven to eleven.

I'd like to picture the boys in their respective bedrooms, under the covers of their beds, with a flashlight and a radio listening to this new music that was about to sweep the nation. Then, one day, Paul heard a singer that would change his life forever. He was riding in the car when the car radio played Elvis Presley. Paul knew immediately that that was what he wanted to do.

However, it was easier said than done. Paul didn't think he had the talent to become the next Elvis Presley, but he kept trying. Art, on the other hand, liked Elvis, but he was more in love with the music. He would practice the songs when he was alone. He especially liked to sing the ballads of the day like "Earth Angel" by the Penguins.

The two kept trying. Every afternoon after school, they would get together and sing at one of their homes. They practiced everything but mostly they learned how to harmonize with each other. Neither was sure if they could make a living singing, but they really wanted to give it a try. The very first time they sang together in public was for a high school yard dance in 1955. I'm assuming a yard dance took place outside. They sang a current popular song "Sh-Boom" which was a number one song for the Crew Cuts in late 1954. The boys were nervous. They didn't know how the kids would react to them, but they didn't have anything to worry about. The kids loved it and applauded loudly. Paul and Art knew that this was where they belonged.

TOM AND JERRY

Art's father had bought him two tape recorders so that he could over dub his voice. Working with these recorders, the two of them started to perfect a sound. They didn't realize that they were creating what would become the Simon & Garfunkel sound. They tried to find places to sing. They would sing at family get-togethers and school events.

But they were boys, also. They did all the things that boys in their early teen years do. They played stickball and basketball and got into fights. They wrestled and played hockey. In the fall of 1955, they started at a new school which was Forest Hills High School. They were in the tenth grade. Now that the summer was over and vacations and play were behind them, they became closer than ever.

Paul's dad thought Paul should learn an instrument and so started him on piano lessons. Try as he might, dad couldn't get Paul interested in the piano, so the project was dropped and instead his younger brother Eddie was taught. Not giving up, dad next bought Paul a guitar. It was a Stadium guitar and cost $25. Stadium is still in business today, only their guitars will cost you much more than that. Looking at their website, the cheapest one I saw was about $400.00. However, guitars have changed a lot in fifty years.

Paul knew he had found his instrument. He took to it right away and was spending six hours a day practicing. Dad got concerned. He told Paul, "I know I got you the guitar, but I meant it as a hobby. You need to do your homework." However, Paul didn't listen. Who needs homework when you're going to be a musician?

Then one day in 1957, a new group began to be heard on the radio. The Everly Brothers released "Bye, Bye Love" as their first hit, reaching number two on the Billboard charts. They followed that up with "Wake Up Little Susie," a number one song and then "All I Have to Do Is Dream" which also went to number one. The important thing here is that Paul and Art were paying attention. The Everlys were a duo, a brother act, and they could really harmonize. Paul and Art, while not brothers, felt like they were brothers in spirit, and they knew they could harmonize. If the Everlys could do it so could they. It wasn't until I started researching this book on S&G that I realized why they brought the Everly Brothers out of retirement to play in their reunion show in 2005. What an impact the Everlys had had on them as kids when they were just starting out!

The guitar allowed Paul to start writing his own songs. His idols were, of course, the Everly Brothers and so he wrote songs that he thought sounded like them. The first song we know about was called "The Girl for Me" and after they copyrighted it, they attempted to sell it to record companies in Manhattan. Of course, no one was buying. The guy at the door would take one look at these two fifteen year olds and tell them to go away. Not interested.

Art and Paul called themselves Tom and Jerry. Now, for my entire life, I have always assumed that they named themselves after the cartoon characters, Tom & Jerry, but not so. The name has nothing to do with the cartoon characters. Paul named himself Jerry Landis after a girl he knew whose last name was Landis. Art named himself Tom Graph after the hobby that he liked most of all. He would spend hours tracking the songs on the radio and graphing their progress on graph paper. The song goes up and the song goes down. Art knew every movement of the hits. I have to admit that I did the exact same thing when I was in high school. I wish I could have made it pay off like Art Garfunkel did.

In 1957, they went to a recording studio where you pay to record a record. It's etched on acetate, and it has to be done in one take because one try is all you get. It has to be right the first time. They recorded two songs: one called "Hey, Schoolgirl" and "Dancin' Wild."

Halfway through the recording session, they were approached by a man named Sid Prosen who told them he liked what he heard. He told them that they kind of sounded like the Everlys. He told them he would make stars out of them. No greater compliment could have been made to them. They immediately signed up with a little record company called Big Records.

Now Big Records didn't amount to much, but it did get them on the charts and it gave the name Tom and Jerry some recognition for a few weeks. They even got to play on Dick Clark's *American Bandstand*. They were on one day when Jerry Lee Lewis was the headline act. They had to follow "The Killer." That was not an easy task, and their performance has pretty much been forgotten by history. Paul said they didn't even get to meet Lewis. He raced into the studio from his limo, did the number, and raced out again, not saying anything to anyone.

After appearing on *Bandstand,* Tom and Jerry were called a cross between the Everly Brothers and the DeJohn Sisters by *Billboard Magazine*. I'm pretty sure they were flattered by the description. That was exactly what they were going for.

But, Paul and Art got just a little taste of what being a celebrity was all about and they liked it. "Hey, Schoolgirl" was not a monster hit, it only peaked at number 59 on the Billboard charts, but it did go Top 10 on the local New York charts. The boys were famous for a short time and were able to play several gigs as a result of that. They played in Cincinnati, Ohio, and in Hartford, Connecticut, but when the record started to slide on the charts, their fame quickly died away.

They recorded two more records for Big Records, but neither one of them were successful (see Discography for titles) and Big couldn't stay in business, so they closed up shop, leaving the boys right back where they started. They did, of course, have one medium hit behind them, but that wasn't enough to provide any real income or career. After all, they were still in high school.

The only thing Paul had to show for his brief sojourn into the music business was a Chevy Impala convertible that he bought with the money he earned from the record. One day, while driving around town (showing off), the car caught on fire, and Paul got out just in time to see the car become engulfed in flames. The money was gone and now the car was gone, also. They decided they should plan their lives as if music wasn't a part of it.

Big Records continued to release Tom & Jerry songs, but none were hits. Strangely, the one song I remember the most is "Baby Talk," ("I am only five years old and my baby's three") which was released in the spring of 1959. However, I can't find any evidence that it hit the charts. It was covered by Jan and Dean, also, and they hit number ten on the Billboard Charts. That's probably why I remember the song so well.

TAKING A BREAK FROM MUSIC

Paul had had Elvis Presley on his mind since the first time he saw him perform. Paul, at fifteen, thought he should have a solo career. Elvis sang alone, so why not him? He never said a word about this to Art. Thus, behind Art's back (Paul didn't see it that way), he recorded a solo record called "True or False." This was recorded under the name of True Taylor. You can listen to the song on YouTube. It sounds to me like a combination of Elvis and Buddy Holly and at this time, Holly wasn't even on the scene.

The song was actually written by Paul's father, Lewis, who, although he didn't like rock and roll and thought his son was wasting his time, saw that this was probably the wave of the future and so supported him in his music.

Art saw it as betrayal. Even though they got back together later and eventually had a successful career as a duo, Art would never feel quite the same about Paul.

Not finding much success after the mediocre reception of "Hey Schoolgirl," the boys settled down and finished high school, graduating in 1958. For a while, they would split up and go their separate ways. (This would happen more than once.) Art decided to attend Columbia University in Manhattan while Paul went a little closer to home at Queens College. They both were creating contingency plans in case they couldn't make a living singing and writing music, although that was still in the back of their minds throughout college. Paul majored in English Literature. I think he enrolled in that major for the wrong reasons: he liked a girl who was an English Lit major, but it served him well later when he started writing music seriously.

Paul earned extra money while going to school by recording demos for recording companies. He was good at imitating other artists and the record company would pay him for the demo. During this time, he met and recorded with a young girl who also attended Queens. She was just starting out like he was and she was cutting her teeth recording demos also. Her name was Carole Klein and she would go on to change her name to Carole King and become one of the greatest writers and recording artists of the Sixties and Seventies.

Paul was able to record a few records during this time. One which I have to mention is "Lone Teen Ranger," a song he wrote and recorded on the Amy label again using the name of Jerry Landis. It just broke into the Top 100 peaking at number 97. This was 1963 and doo wop was pretty much dead by this time. The song has the old Fifties style to it, and it is fun to listen to today, but I can understand why it wasn't a hit.

In 1959, he got a contract with MGM records and recorded several records under the name Jerry Landis. None of them did very much but if you search YouTube for the name Jerry Landis you will find most of them and they are fun to listen to after all these years. He also sang background for other groups, like the Mystics. He sang on their version of "All Through the Night" which didn't really do anything, but it was giving Paul experience.

This was a tough time for the both of them. Art and Paul worked together and they worked separately. This was the age of unrest among young people. They knew things were not right in the world, but no one knew exactly what to do about it. We were involved in the Vietnam War and nobody liked that, especially the college students.

Art eventually decided to major in architecture, also pretty much for all the wrong reasons. He had read a book by Ayn Rand called *The Fountainhead* which is a huge novel. I read it myself in the sixties.

The main character is an architect, so Art thought it would be cool to be an architect.

Art was soon bored with architecture and school in general and decided to take a break. He had heard that interesting things were happening in California, so he travelled to San Francisco. College kids, by this time, were pretty tired of Fifties style rock and roll and were looking for something new. The era of folk music had begun in California and it featured artists like a new, bright, young kid named Bob Dylan who was just breaking onto the scene.

Back in 1958, the Kingston Trio had had a number one hit with "Tom Dooley." By the early Sixties, that sound was being heard more and more on college campuses. Besides Bob Dylan, there was Joan Baez and Pete Seeger. A new group Peter, Paul, and Mary were making their mark. All of this really appealed to Art, so he arranged to record a song using the name of Artie Garr, dropping the Tom Graph name forever. Art longed to write songs like Paul did, but he was never very good at it. Therefore, he ended up singing other people's work. He concentrated on standards and would revive them and bring them up to date. His voice was so pure, he was able to sell it. However, he did write one song called "Private World," which, if you listen to it on YouTube, sounds an awful lot like "Greenfields," a big hit by the Brothers Four, another folk group of the Sixties.

The song didn't go anywhere, the Vietnam War was getting into full swing, and he worried about getting drafted. Therefore, he did the only thing he could do (short of skipping out of the country altogether): he went back to college. He returned to New York and Columbia to resume his education.

Paul didn't have to worry about military service since the powers that be had graded him 4F because of a heart murmur.

When Art returned from the West Coast, he literally ran into Paul on the streets. It was almost inevitable since they only lived three blocks

James Hoag

apart. Paul showed Art all the new songs that he had written, and Art became excited. It was time to get back together and give it another try.

They got a job playing at Gerde's Folk City, a club in the Village in New York (using the name "Kane and Garr.") This was really the first time they sang together that they really felt it and realized that this was something special. Now all they had to do was convince others that they were special, too.

SIGNING ON WITH COLUMBIA

Consequently, Paul arranged an appointment with Tom Wilson, who was a producer for Columbia Records, and asked him for an audition. Wilson agreed, and the boys came to Columbia to play for the decision makers of the company. While Columbia and Wilson were not blown away by the guys, they did like them enough to invite them back for another try.

This time, they sang four songs for them which again didn't really impress them, except for "He Was My Brother." Tom Wilson was black and immediately related to the song's theme about the fight for civil rights in the south. The problem was, Wilson wanted the song for another group which was signed to Columbia. Paul said, "No. I want to record the songs ourselves." Wilson said O.K., so they got started, but things were moving very slowly.

Paul continued to write for a yet unnamed album. Paul is a very slow writer, and it was taking months. He had started with a melody that would later become "The Sound of Silence" but couldn't come up with what came next. He had some of the words but not all of them.

Therefore, in the fall of 1963, Paul decided to go to France for some inspiration. He spent a couple of months in Paris wandering the streets, his guitar strapped to his back, and playing the part of the wanderer. Sometimes, he would put the open guitar case on the ground, and he would stand near-by and sing, hoping people would drop a few coins in the case.

While in Paris, he met a man who would have an important impact on his life. His name was Dave McCausland and he ran a club back in London. He told Paul to come to London and look him up, so Paul did just that. There, he met Kathy Chitty who would be his first real love. They would be together for several years but never married.

While in France, Paul wrote several new songs and tweaked a few he had already written, which he played for Art when he got home. One song was the aforementioned "He Was My Brother" and if you haven't heard it, find it on YouTube and listen. There is some dispute as to who this song is really about, but it appears to be about a friend of Paul's who he knew in college named Andrew Goodman. Goodman had gone to Mississippi as a civil rights activist and was killed by members of the Ku Klux Klan. The song itself was written about two years before Goodman was killed, but after the murder, Paul revived the song and claimed it was now about Goodman.

Another song, "Sparrow," is classic Simon & Garfunkel. It's a little sad but very typical of the music of the early Sixties and has the Simon & Garfunkel sound. Also, Paul wrote "Bleecker Street," a song about the famous street in Greenwich Village in New York City. These are all examples of the sound of S&G when they were first starting out and all three songs would appear on their first album *Wednesday Morning 3 A.M.*

Paul was having a ball in England, playing at all the local clubs, and dating Kathy. Art, on the other hand, was still studying. He had realized that Architecture was not what he wanted, so he had switched to Mathematics and planned to become a teacher. I can't say for sure because I have not talked to the guys, but it seems to me that Art was not that confident that he could earn a living playing and singing. Paul, on the other hand, moved ahead as if he were already a success.

"THE SOUND OF SILENCE"

Then, on November 22, 1963, something happened which would change everything for Paul and Art, although they didn't know it at the time. President Kennedy was assassinated on that day in Dallas, Texas. America would never be the same. Paul would never be the same. The grief he felt was tangible. It was during this time and probably as a direct result of the assassination that Paul finished what would be his most famous song, "The Sound of Silence."

Paul said later that the song was just a cry of post-adolescent angst, but the song spoke to the generation of the Sixties. I have heard it said that this song was the anthem of the Sixties but, of course, that didn't happen until later. It took Paul about four months to write the song. He started with the music and had that down pretty well but couldn't come up with the lyrics. Then one day in February of 1964, he was sitting in his bathroom, strumming the guitar (the acoustics in the bathroom were great) and the words came to him.

It's interesting to note that the song was originally "The Sounds of Silence" (the word **Sounds** is plural) and if you look on the first album they produced that is the way it's spelled. But later, the "s" is dropped and it just became "The Sound of Silence."

After the album was done, they sat down and tried to decide on a name for the group. Tom & Jerry was out. Their sound was much different than it was in the Fifties. They battered around a number of different choices and finally decided to just go with their real names, Simon & Garfunkel. Now, that may not seem like a big deal today, but it was then. Their names were blatantly Jewish, and the record company wasn't sure the public would buy from Jewish performers. After all, Bob Dylan had changed his name from his real name of Robert Zimmerman for just that reason.

However, Paul said he wanted to be truthful with the public. They would stick with their own names and so it was decided, from then on, they would be known as Simon & Garfunkel.

They had recorded the album and when they were done, they felt really good about it. The album was released on October 19, 1964. They sat back and waited to see what would happen. In a word, nothing happened.

In the summer of 1964, after the album was finished, but before it was released, Paul went back to England and back to Kathy. In America, he was just one of many musicians who were trying to make it big. In England, he was an American who could sing and that made him special. He found he could get about as much work as he wanted. He worked in several different clubs and kept busy. He renewed his relationship with Kathy Chitty; life was good.

After school finished for the year, Art decided to join him and so, during the summer of 1964, the two rented motor scooters and rode all over Europe and England taking in the sights. To me, this is the perfect way to spend a summer when you are a college aged person. I look back on those days and wish I had been brave enough to do something like that.

Unfortunately, the fun had to come to an end sometime. Fall was approaching, and Art needed to go back to school. The album was finished, but Art felt he still needed to cover himself in case his career in the music business never came to pass. And, it almost didn't.

Consequently, when the album was released in October, Paul waited to see if they would have a hit. When he had come back from England, he had brought Kathy with him and the two of them spent the fall driving around America with Paul showing her the country. Paul did a lot of travelling that year.

When nothing happened, and the album sold a grand total of only about 3000 copies, Paul said, "I'm outta here" and returned once again to England.

However, it was during this trip that things began to happen. Paul, feeling dejected and rejected by the record buying public, spent some time by himself and wrote one of his most famous songs, "Homeward Bound." "Every stop is neatly planned for a poet and a one-man band." It's a sad song and reflects the way Paul was feeling at the time. Later, it would become a big hit, but that time was still in the future.

Now, Paul was being noticed in England. It was easier to get work, and people were recognizing his name. They wanted to know where they could buy his music. Of course, his first album wasn't available yet, so he called Columbia and asked about recording an album in England. The timing was exactly right as Columbia wanted to break into the British market. After all, the Beatles had taken over America, so it was only right that we go over there, so, Columbia agreed to let Paul record a solo album, and the result was *The Paul Simon Songbook* which was released in 1965 by CBS Records in Great Britain (owned by Columbia.) Paul was able to record the album very quickly, not like the time it took in the States. He stood in front of a microphone and sang. Most of the songs on the album were recorded in one take.

The album has one big thing going for it. The cover shows Paul and Kathy sitting on the cobblestones on a London street. Now, we know what Kathy looked like in 1965. The reprints that are available today also have this picture. The album also contains the first appearance of "I Am a Rock" which wasn't released in the United States until over a year later. Columbia tried to release the album in the United States in 1969, but Paul objected to the release, and it was quickly pulled from the stores. If you were fortunate enough to get a copy during the couple days it was on sale, you probably have a collector's item.

It was also released as part of a box set in 1981 and then again on CD in 2004, so it is available today. You can get it on Amazon for about $7, but it's a reprint. The original will cost you much more than that.

Paul was having a moderate amount of success in Britain, but the British people thought he was arrogant. He came across during interviews as being very conceited, and Paul admits that that was the way he felt. Art came to England in the summer of 1965 on a break from school and the two tried to find some work. While they could always find a place to sing, nobody was paying much attention. Back home in America, the team assigned to Simon & Garfunkel was disbanded and given other jobs. It seemed as if the career of S&G was over.

THEN LIGHTNING STRUCK

In the late summer of 1965, a disc jockey in Boston, Massachusetts, on station WBZ started playing a song that he rather liked. The song was "The Sound of Silence" and amazingly, people started to call in and request it be played more. It was placed into rotation and played more often and still they got requests to play it even more. This was the summer of 1965. To this day, no one is sure what the public heard that they hadn't heard before but suddenly the song was a hit. Tom Wilson found out that it was being played on a couple stations in Florida as well. Up to then (September, 1965), it only existed on the *Wednesday Morning 3 A.M.* album. A single was quickly cut and even though the song was meant to be done acoustically with a guitar and the boys' voices (as it was on the album), when the song was re-recorded for the single, Tom Wilson dubbed drums and an electric guitar in over the guys work unbeknownst to either Paul or Art. Needless to say, they were not happy about it.

Check out the flip side of the original single record. It's called "We've Got a Groovy Thing Goin'" and, to me, is a completely different kind of song than "The Sound of Silence." But, luckily, no one paid much attention to the B-side. It was "The Sound of Silence" that everyone wanted to hear. At first, Paul was really irritated that Wilson had added the drums and such to the arrangement but the more he heard it, the more he liked it. Art thought it was OK right from the beginning. They had, literally, invented a new sound in music, something called "folk-rock."

The song entered the Billboard Top 40 and on New Year's Day, 1966, it hit number one. Simon & Garfunkel were about to become a household name. If you have a hit record, you do two things (at least), you start promoting the original album and you think about cutting a new album. Tom Wilson had moved on by this time, so Columbia assigned a new producer to S&G named Bob Johnston. Johnston was also Bob Dylan's producer, and the company thought that he was a good fit for Paul and Art. They gave them three weeks to get a new album ready.

Well, Paul didn't need three weeks. He already had the material written. His *Songbook* album in Great Britain had pretty much bombed, but he knew he could still use some of the songs, especially when it would be both him and Art singing in harmony. That should improve the music.

From *Songbook*, they took "I Am a Rock," "A Most Peculiar Man," "Leaves That Are Green," "April Come She Will," and "Kathy's Song," all re-recorded with the distinctive S&G sound. On *Songbook*, it had just been Paul and a guitar. Now, the songs received the full treatment. To take advantage of the new hit they had on their hands, the album was called *Sounds of Silence*. Of the eleven songs on the album, the title song, of course, had been recorded for their first album, *Wednesday Morning 3 A.M.* Also, the flip side of the hit "We've Got a Groovy Thing Goin'" was included. A song which had been recorded back in April, 1965 was also included, "Somewhere They Can't Find Me," but everything else was recorded between December 13th and December 22nd of 1965. That's ten days to record an album, quite a change from the first album which took months to complete.

The album *Sounds of Silence* was released January 17, 1966 and reached number 21 on the Billboard album charts. It was Gold in Canada and 3xPlatinum in the United States. Columbia was in a hurry, however, and wanted to strike while the iron was hot. This was the era of the single, and they needed another one right away. Thus, they took the unusual step of recording a single which does not appear on the *Sounds of Silence* album, a song Paul wrote and recorded in England called "Homeward Bound."

"Homeward Bound" would appear on album number three *Parsley, Sage, Rosemary, and Thyme* which wouldn't be released until later in the year. "Homeward Bound" is a lonely song. "I'm sittin' in a railway station/Got a ticket for my destination." You can feel the loneness and the desire to get back home in the words and in the music. Paul missed his girlfriend when he wrote the song. There is some dispute as to exactly where Paul was when he wrote it, but the consensus is that he was at Widnes which is located in Cheshire, England. There is, indeed, a train station there, and they have mounted a plaque in the area where people wait for the Liverpool train. The plaque commemorates the song "Homeward Bound."

"Homeward Bound" was released in February of 1966 and peaked at number five on the Billboard Hot 100 Charts. By now, the album was out and they could follow up that with their third hit, "I Am a Rock" which is from the *Sounds of Silence* album. "I Am a Rock" would peak at number three on the charts and become their third Top 10 song in a row. However, it would be two years before they hit the Top 10 again.

If you listen to several Simon & Garfunkel songs back to back, you will see that they are talking directly to the young people of the Sixties. Paul's songs were called alienating and isolating, but this was how the youth of the Sixties felt (and to some extent, still do). Listen to the lyrics of the first three hits that they had, "The Sound of Silence," "Hello darkness my old friend," and then "Homeward Bound" which I've already excerpted a line from and "I Am a Rock." "I am a rock/I am an island" and then this: "I have no need of friendship/Friendship causes pain." This is pretty depressing stuff but when you listen to it, surprisingly, you don't feel depressed. You feel uplifted and good about the world. That was the genius of Paul Simon.

Having had over 10 years in the music business (off and on), Art and Paul knew that the kind of music they sang was not really in the same league as most of the rock and roll of the day. When they were booked to sing with The Four Seasons and Chuck Berry, they knew they had to force a change. They needed a good manager, so they hired a man named Mort Lewis, who was a manager only to the top stars of the time. Lewis understood them and realized that the college crowd was where they would fit in the best, and he was right.

They started playing the campuses around New York and other areas. Art was still going to school, trying to get a graduate degree, so this fit great with him as most of their performing was done on weekends and that gave Art time to attend classes during the week and record when possible. Lewis also felt that a pattern of "underexposure" would be good for the duo. If the public saw too much of them, they wouldn't have remained as mysterious. This actually increased record sales and drew more people to the concerts that they did perform.

During the summer of 1966, a group called Cyrkle recorded a song that Paul had written a couple years earlier in England with a member of the Seekers, Bruce Woodley. The song "Red Rubber Ball" was a number two hit for the Cyrkle in the United States. The song continues Paul's reputation as an isolationist, as it's about a guy who is breaking up with his girlfriend and everything is going to be all right.

"Parsley, Sage, Rosemary, and Thyme"

Meanwhile, they started work on their next album and their next single which would come from that album. Album number three, *Parsley, Sage, Rosemary, and Thyme,* would be released in October of 1966 and had the advantage of having one big hit already out, "Homeward Bound." However, that would be the best any song from the album would do. The name of the album comes from the words of the leading song on the A-side of the album, "Scarborough Fair/Canticle."

There are a lot of interesting things to be said about *Parsley, Sage, Rosemary, and Thyme*. It would have three hits come from the album, the first being "The Dangling Conversation." The song goes back to England, again, where Paul remembers sitting on the floor of his flat with his girlfriend, reading the poetry of Emily Dickinson and Robert Frost. Once again, the song is about loss. After three Top five records in a row, "The Dangling Conversation" only reached number 25 on the Billboard charts. This was a disappointment to Paul and Art, but they kept moving forward.

Even though the guys had had three big hits, they continued to work as mostly opening acts for other groups. But, at least, their manager was pairing them up with groups that were more like them. Groups like the Mamas and the Papas and the Lovin' Spoonful.

Their music caught the ear of Hollywood director Mike Nichols who was looking for someone to write the music for a new movie that he was filming called *The Graduate*. Nichols felt that Paul Simon's music would make a great fit for the movie. Columbia agreed as they saw it as another profit avenue for the guys. The plot of the movie seemed to be perfect for Paul and Art, as it dealt with a young man (Dustin Hoffman) and an older woman, Mrs. Robinson, (Anne

Bancroft) who flirts with him throughout the movie. The only problem with working on the movie would be that Paul had to adhere to specific schedules and deliver his music on time. Paul was used to taking his time and was known as something of a perfectionist.

Parsley, Sage, Rosemary, and Thyme took several months longer than it should have for that very reason. Paul would obsess over each song until he had it exactly like he wanted it. That made it particularly upsetting when "The Dangling Conversion" was not the hit he thought it should be.

Two songs I have to mention from the album were not hits as singles but still managed to be heard. "The 59th Street Bridge Song" (or better known as "Feeling Groovy") was a little out of character with the rest of the album. It has a bouncy, feel good quality about it that makes you glad to be alive. You might say, "I remember that song; it was played on the radio all the time." You are probably remembering the version of the song that was recorded by the group Harper's Bizarre, a group out of California who recorded a cover of the song. It reached number thirteen on the Top 40, but S&G's version didn't chart at all.

The other song that interests me is called "7 O'Clock News/Silent Night" and is a very simple song but very powerful. It simply consists of Paul and Art singing the traditional Christmas song "Silent Night," while a 1966 news cast is playing in the background. As the song goes along, the news cast gets louder and louder, effectively drowning out the spirituality of the "Silent Night." I just listened to the song, and I am particularly impressed by how the news hasn't really changed much in forty years. Only the names have changed, but the news still sounds the same as it did in 1966. If you'd like to reminisce about the events that shaped our nation in the mid-Sixties, go back and listen to "7 O'Clock News/Silent Night."

As is the habit of record companies, the next single had not been released in an album yet. "A Hazy Shade of Winter" was released as a single in November of 1966, about a year and a half before the album that would contain the song came out. That album was *Bookends*, which we'll talk about later. The song is another in the line of somber pieces done by S&G, except this one is a little more upbeat, with a strong drum beat behind it. In 1987, the group, The Bangles, choose to cover the song for the soundtrack of *Less Than Zero*. Their version is much more rock oriented and edgier, although I like it almost as much as the original.

Even though Art mentioned that he felt that the career of Simon & Garfunkel began with the album *Parsley, Sage, Rosemary, and Thyme,* it also marked what I believe to be the first cracks that were appearing in the relationship. They had one basic problem. Paul did most, if not all, of the work and Art seemed to just go along for the ride. No one could dispute that Simon & Garfunkel would not have been the same without Art. Both did have successful solo careers after they split up, but neither one alone would produce what they did together.

However, it did cause friction. Paul got most of the royalties from the records since he wrote all of the songs. He also got 75% of the revenue from concert performances. I think Art resented this a little, and it would take a few more years before things came to a head and the actual separation occurred.

The Drug Years

In March of 1967, they released their next single, "At the Zoo." Some people see this as an innocent children's song. Paul even wrote a children's book which featured all the animals mentioned in the song. However, keep in mind that this was the last half of the decade of the Sixties. Drugs was the prevalent topic in a lot of popular songs of that day. The Beatles were getting very psychedelic and there were many songs about drugs. "At the Zoo" was Paul's ode to the drugs that he and most other performers were taking on a regular basis.

The songs that Paul had written years before in England had run out, and he was now faced with the task of writing new ones. Having been a drug user (primarily marijuana and hashish), Paul was not a stranger to the drug world, but things really came to a head in 1967. Keep in mind that the summer of 1967 was infamously called "The Summer of Love." Paul says he was high as much as six months out of the year.

One highlight of 1967 was the Monterey Pop Festival which occurred in Monterey, California, from June 16th to June 18th. Paul and Art, even though they had taken drugs on a regular basis, felt like fish out of water in the presence of such people as Jimi Hendrix and Janis Joplin. This was the concert that put these people on the map. Simon & Garfunkel seemed tame compared to them. However, the people loved them anyway.

"At the Zoo" did well on the charts, peaking at number sixteen. It would be another year before they would return to the Top 10, but things were going along fairly well. Paul and Art and, most importantly, Columbia, thought they were doing fine. In the public's eye, they were a class act and consistently hitting the Top Twenty was quite an accomplishment.

They started work on their next album, *Bookends*. Some of the songs were already done and had been released as singles. The next single released (which would end up on *Bookends*) was "Fakin' It." The song was not as big a hit as some of their previous songs, only peaking at number 23. A couple of interesting facts are related to this song. The song actually runs three minutes and fourteen seconds. Radio Stations, however, wanted songs that were less than three minutes, so Paul "faked it" and had Columbia print 2:74 on the label of the record, so it would get more airplay.

Also, the flip side of "Fakin' It" is called "You Don't Know Where Your Interest Lies" and was, at the time, the only song S&G released on a 45 record that did not exist on any album. It was not included in *Bookends* or any other album until many years later when the label started putting together *Greatest Hits* albums.

"MRS. ROBINSON"

I hope you haven't forgotten about *The Graduate* which Paul was supposed to write original music for. Mike Nichols sure hadn't forgotten and was calling Paul nearly every day wanting his music, but Paul was busy touring and trying to write music for the next album. Nichols was very upset with him and started to use Paul Simon music from earlier times to play over the movie so that they could get the mood of the music if and when Paul came through with original music.

Unfortunately, Paul never really came through. He did manage to put together the start of a song, and he mentioned it one day to Nichols. Nichols about blew a gasket, as you can imagine. "You have a song about Mrs. Robinson?" he asked incredulously. Paul admitted that he did, but it wasn't actually about Mrs. Robinson; it was about Mrs. Roosevelt and Joe DiMaggio and wasn't done yet.

In actuality, he had one line, "And here's to you Joe DiMaggio/A Nation turns its lonely eyes to you." That was it. Paul and Art continued to work on the song and finally changed the name to "Mrs. Robinson," and everyone was happy. Mike Nichols reworked much of the music in the soundtrack so that the music appeared to be coming from the viewpoint of Benjamin Braddock (played by a young, unknown Dustin Hoffman.)

Unfortunately, while Paul did eventually finish "Mrs. Robinson," the version that appears on the soundtrack is very anemic. To hear the song in its full glory, you need to listen to the version that ended up on the *Bookends* album. The songs that stand out to me on the soundtrack are "The Sound of Silence" which is just their original hit and "Scarborough Fair/Canticle" which was on the *Parsley, Sage,*

Rosemary, and Thyme album which had been recorded two years prior to the movie being released.

"Scarborough Fair/Canticle" was released as a single in February of 1968 and peaked at number eleven, becoming their highest charting song since "I Am a Rock" in 1966. Striking while the iron was hot, Columbia next released "Mrs. Robinson" as a single with the version that appeared on *Bookends*. The single would go all the way to the top and become the second number one of their career. This song, more than anything else, cemented Simon & Garfunkel into the minds and hearts of the record buying public and the annals of rock and roll music.

Bookends would reach number one in both the United States and Great Britain. The album contains more recognizable music by Simon & Garfunkel than any other, in my opinion. Paul and Art were both a little worried about two albums being out at the same time. They thought it might dilute the sales and both would suffer. They didn't have to worry. Both albums hit number one. This was easy since *The Graduate* had been released in January of 1968 and *Bookends* wasn't released until April, so that created enough of a buffer between the albums that both could become hits. They both ended up selling 2xplatinum. It's interesting to note that it was *Bookends* that pushed *The Graduate* out of first place. Simon & Garfunkel were now officially super stars.

Bookends was well received by the critics and by the public. Several of the songs had previously been released as singles, but no one seemed to care.

Paul was asked to write music for several more movies and Broadway shows. Leonard Bernstein even asked him to help score a mass that he had written. Unfortunately, Paul didn't work well under deadlines. His experience with Mike Nichols told him that he had to work on his own time table that he couldn't be told he needed something done by a certain time and then expect to do it. Paul was his own man and ran by his own schedule.

This attitude would be part of why he and Art would break up just two years later.

"Catch-22"

Art met Mike Nichols again one day on the streets of New York, and Nichols asked him if he'd like to be in the next movie that he was directing. The movie *Catch-22*, based on the book, would be another major blockbuster. Art had secretly been harboring a desire to get into acting. A lot of other rock performers had gone the Hollywood route (most notably Elvis Presley), and Art thought he would like to give it a try.

Nichols told him he had a part for Paul as well and both Paul and Art became very excited at the idea of going to Hollywood to be in a movie. The parts were not big, but it could be a start. Unfortunately, Art's role was kept and Paul's part was cut from the movie, so this served to further drive a wedge between the two.

They continued to perform, and Paul continued to try to write new songs for a new album that was as yet unnamed. Everything seemed cordial on the surface; however, underneath bad feelings were starting to fester. The two just didn't seem to be as close of friends as they used to be.

1968 was a rough year for the country. Vietnam was escalating, and Lyndon Johnson decided not to run for re-election for the Presidency, opening the door for Richard Nixon to come in. Both Martin Luther King and Robert Kennedy were assassinated that year, and America was reeling from all the unrest. However, for Simon & Garfunkel, it was their best year yet. They were number one selling artists, everyone was talking about them, and they had more money than they could spend.

"Mrs. Robinson" spent three weeks at number one as a single and twelve weeks in total on the charts, pretty much dominating the summer of 1968. Things were good on the outside; it was only under the surface that trouble was brewing.

1969 arrived to find Art in Mexico mostly sitting around waiting for his turn to film his parts in *Catch-22*. That left Paul at home to grumble and get more and more upset with Art. In March, however, the Grammy awards were presented and in those days, the people nominated knew who the winner was before the ceremony actually took place, so Paul and Art arranged to fly to Hollywood to participate in the Grammy Award presentation. They won the Grammy for Best Record of the Year for "Mrs. Robinson" and the records it was up against were power houses like "Hey Jude" by the Beatles and "Wichita Lineman" by Glen Campbell as well as others.

They also received a Grammy for Best Contemporary Pop Vocal Performance by a Group. Paul received a personal Grammy for his work on the Soundtrack of *The Graduate*. Thus, for one night at least, all was right with the world. Then, Art returned to Mexico to work on the movie, and Paul went home to New York to work on his next hit.

"THE BOXER"

That hit would be "The Boxer" which was written and recorded in the third quarter of 1969. This is easily one of my favorite S&G songs. It makes me feel good every time I hear it, even though it is a little sad. I once had a friend, and we would play a game (nerds that we were). We would try to come up with songs that had lyrics but yet never actually said the name of the song in the lyrics. There was always a battle over "The Boxer," for those exact words are never said in the song. If you listen close they sing "a boxer" which is slightly different.

It took over 100 hours to record this five minute song. It was recorded in several locations, including Nashville and, of all places, St. Paul's Chapel in New York City. My favorite part of the song is the instrumental which is much more powerful in "The Boxer" than in previous works; especially, the sound of the bass harmonica that is heard at a couple of points in the song.

Some people thought that "The Boxer" was a jab at Bob Dylan. Paul and Dylan had been feuding a little and when they heard the chorus of "Lie la lie" sung over and over, they thought this was Paul calling Dylan a liar. Not so, Paul says. The chorus is sung that way because when Paul wrote the song, he couldn't think of any good words to put in for the chorus, so he just sang nonsense words. Later, during recording, it sounded so good that way, that they just left it and he never did write any words for the chorus.

It amazes me how people are always trying to interpret words in a song to mean something different than what they really mean. Sometimes song writers just write words because they sound cool or they fit the measure of the song. There is no hidden meaning and if you play the music backwards and think you hear something sinister, then it's probably just your imagination. The writer was just trying to write a good song.

"The Boxer" only reached number seven on the Billboard charts, but it should have been a number one. I think it was that good. It would be the only single released in 1969. Paul later said that the song was really about him. It was about fighting your way up to the top after starting at the bottom. It reflected the loneness he felt since Art was gone most of the time.

FEMALE COMPANIONSHIP

In 1969, Paul again fell in love; this time with a woman named Peggy Harper who happened to be married to their manager, Mort Lewis. This caused some problems, but Paul was determined to be with Peggy, so Peggy asked Lewis for a divorce so she and Paul could get married.

Art also met someone. He accidently ran into an old friend from college who had also studied architecture but never finished the schooling. Her name was Linda Grossman, and they met on the streets of New York one day during a break from filming. They were immediately smitten with each other, and Art liked Linda very much.

In order to be together more, Paul and Art rented a house in Los Angeles and they and Peggy moved in. They set up a studio in one of the rooms, and it was there that they recorded a song which took S&G back to their early days when making music was fun. "Cecilia" was born in that house and made everyone feel good. Some people say that "Cecilia" is a reference to St Cecilia who is the patron saint of music in the Catholic Church, but I think it was just a rhythm that Paul liked and words that he liked and no hidden meaning is meant at all. "Cecilia" would be released later in April of 1970 after their huge hit "Bridge Over Troubled Water" which we'll talk about next.

Listen to the rhythm of "Cecilia." Hear the beat right toward the beginning of the song. That sound was largely the result of Paul and Art slapping the legs of their jeans inside an echo chamber. They really liked the sound that made. It's certainly unique, and "Cecilia" wouldn't be the same without it.

Now, I haven't found this in any other writing, but I remember in the town I was living in when this song was released that the station would not play it at first. They didn't like the line about making love up in the bedroom and then the singer gets up to wash his face only to find that someone had taken his place. Now, this was 1970 and the age of drugs and promiscuity had already happened in the Sixties, but my local station still felt squeamish about playing the song. Fortunately, public opinion prevailed, and the song was played. It eventually reached number four on the Billboard charts.

Even though they only had one hit in 1969, they were extremely busy that year. Art was still working on *Catch-22* (it was dragging on forever), and Paul was busy with a new girlfriend and trying to write songs for the *Bridge Over Troubled Water* album. Someone approached them and offered them a place in this then unknown celebration which was planned for August of 1969 called Woodstock, but they had to decline; they were just too busy.

The complexity of the new music caused further problems between Paul and Art. One of the songs that Paul wrote for the new album was written while Art was away working on the movie in Mexico. It's called "The Only Living Boy in New York" and mentions both Tom (a reference to their days as Tom & Jerry) and Mexico (where Art was working at the time). Another song for the new album was "Why Don't You Write Me" which is an up tempo fun sounding song but underscores just how lonely Paul was (they were actually living in Los Angeles at the time.)

Lastly, Paul wrote (reportedly at Art's request) a tribute to the famous architect Frank Lloyd Wright who had died in 1959. "So Long Frank Lloyd Wright" on the surface is a tribute to the great man, but many believe that Paul is again writing about Art. You might remember that Art started out majoring in Architecture in college, even though he never finished the degree in that field. Paul is saying so long to Art because he knew that their days were numbered.

If Art recognized any of this, I'm not sure, but I tend to believe that he knew exactly what was going on. Their relationship was coming to a close.

James Hoag

"Bridge Over Troubled Water"

But it wasn't quite dead, yet. They still had one more album to release, and they were up for a television special in the fall of 1969. During the summer of 1969, Paul was working on what he considered his best effort yet, "Bridge Over Troubled Water." Paul said later than when he would lay down a verse of the song, it seemed almost like a spiritual experience. Tears would come to his eyes. He was positive it was the best thing he had ever written, and he wanted Art to sing it solo. No harmony on this song.

Paul had always been interested in Gospel music and remembered a song from 1958 called "Mary Don't You Weep," a gospel song done by Claude Jeter who most people don't know unless you're really familiar with Fifties Gospel music. Yet, a line from that song "I'll be a bridge over deep water, if you trust in me" had stuck with Paul all those years, and he finally had a chance to use it in a song.

Art came back from working on *Catch-22* in Mexico and when he first heard it, he didn't really like it that much. Paul was crushed. They argued about the song for days until, finally, Art agreed to sing the song solo. This underscored how they had separated on what each felt was good music. Art liked "Bridge," he just didn't think it was Paul's best work.

The song originally had only two verses, but Art and producer Roy Halee thought it needed a little more, so they convinced Paul to write a third verse. By now, Paul was married to Peggy, and he had noticed a gray hair. The words "Sail on, silver girl" are a reference to Peggy, his wife.

The song was released in late January of 1970 and about a month later, on February 28, it hit number one where it stayed for six weeks, easily becoming the biggest hit of their career. The song also hit number one in England, Canada, France, and New Zealand. The song "Bridge Over Troubled Water" won the 1970 Grammy for Record of the Year and the album of the same name won the Grammy for Album of the Year (awarded in March of 1971). *Rolling Stone Magazine* rates the song as number 47 of the 500 Greatest Songs of All Time.

"Bridge" was first heard by the public during a television special that aired on November 30th, 1969. Now this is an interesting show. It was originally sponsored by AT&T (Bell Telephone) and when they saw the tapes of what Simon & Garfunkel planned to put on the air, they were very upset. They felt the music was "too political." During the playing of "Bridge Over Troubled Water," Paul showed scenes in the life of John Kennedy and his brother Robert as well as that of Martin Luther King. AT&T complained that they were all Democrats and that would offend the right wing viewers in the country.

The discussion went on for weeks until, finally, AT&T pulled out of the project, leaving CBS and S&G without a sponsor. AT&T did sell the show to another sponsor, and the show was aired on time. AT&T took a great loss on the show. The show was never repeated and has never, to my knowledge, been shown anywhere else. However, as with all things in the age of the internet, you can find the show in its entirety on YouTube. Just search for "Songs for America Simon & Garfunkel" and you'll find it. It also gives you a very good look at what the boys looked like in 1970. Oh, how times have changed.

The next single released from the *Bridge Over Troubled Water* album was "Cecilia" which has already been discussed.

After "Cecilia" was "El Condor Pasa (If I Could)" which is based on an 18th Century Peruvian folk song that Paul heard when he was living in Paris, years earlier. As usually happens with albums, this single did not do as well as the others before it. "El Condor Pasa" only reached eighteen on the charts, and it would be five years before they charted on the Top 40 again.

The song on *Bridge* which personifies the eventual breakup of Simon & Garfunkel is "So Long Frank Lloyd Wright" which is said to be the only public announcement of the breakup. At the end of the song, Art is singing, "So Long, So Long" over and over and at about the three minute mark you can hear very faintly in the background, Paul sing out "So long, already, Artie." I had to play the song again to hear it. You'll miss it if you're not looking for it, but it's there.

I think the most poignant song on the album is "Song for the Asking" which is the last song on the B-side of the album. This causes some to say that this was the last S&G song of their career. If you listen to the words, it seems that Paul is trying to make amends. He really doesn't want it to end. He says he is willing to change, but Art doesn't get the message. Not soon after their tour and live concerts for *Bridge Over Troubled Water*, Art accepted a new role in a movie: another Mike Nichols film, this one called *Carnal Knowledge* which would begin production soon. This was the final nail in the coffin. This really signaled the end of Simon & Garfunkel.

Just a few more words about the breakup since everything I've written so far has led up to this. Paul and Art did tour together for much of the remainder of the year 1970. Art was accepted into the movie business and secretly harbored a desire to become a movie star, putting this ahead of the music. The Simon & Garfunkel act had always put Paul Simon first (even in the name). Art Garfunkel always felt like he was second string to Paul's stardom. Paul did the writing and the recording and Art seemed to come in as an afterthought and join him in the harmonies. Paul was the leader.

Now, Art was doing something Paul could not do or did not want to do: act. Art was suddenly in the spotlight, and Paul was relegated to the background. This upset Paul greatly, and he resented it. It was a miracle that the two stayed together as long as they did. The final curtain was a concert in Queens, just a few blocks from where they grew up. They had come full circle, and they came out on stage wearing ball caps and jeans, just the two of them, no orchestra or any other instruments except a piano. They sang all the hits. The last song they did was "Bridge Over Troubled Water" (hence the piano) and then, without a goodbye, they walked off the stage. That would be the last time they sang together for more than ten years, except for one brief meeting two years later. An era was over.

James Hoag

PAUL SIMON ALONE

Paul's biggest problem was that no one believed that the two were really finished. He couldn't get anyone to take him seriously. He settled down and tried to figure out what he was going to do next. The Grammy's in March of 1971 brought the two together briefly for one night. The problem was, no one knew they were really apart. This was the first year that the Grammy's hadn't been announced before the event and so it was a surprise to the guys when they won Record of the Year, Album of the Year, and Song of the Year (the top three awards.) They also won three additional Grammies in lesser categories, six in all that year, and they appeared on stage together. *Bridge Over Troubled Water* was the biggest album in history up until that time. The year of its release, 1970, Paul Simon received $7 million just for the fact that he had written the album. That doesn't count any of the other monies collected from touring, etc.

Paul decided that he needed to get right back to work. The problem was, he had melodies in his head with no words to go with them, so he kept working. He wanted to get away from the style of Simon & Garfunkel and establish his own sound. He wanted people to know when they heard the song that they were listening to Paul Simon, not Simon & Garfunkel.

He released his first post-S&G album in January of 1972, and it was the self-titled *Paul Simon*. If the public was still in denial about the breakup, this would settle it once and for all. Paul was recording by himself. Most people see this album as a bridge between *Bridge Over Troubled Water* and what followed in Paul's career. The songs are personal and autobiographical and reflect a lot of the anxiety that Paul was feeling at the time. He and Peggy were having problems, and this worried him. (They would later divorce in 1975.)

The album reached number four on the album charts in the United States and number one in England as well as four other countries. It seems the public had forgiven him, but most of the critics didn't think it was all that good. They didn't think it reached the level of *Bridge Over Troubled Water* or *The Sounds of Silence*. They were looking for the same thing, but Paul was writing something different which was exactly the way he wanted it. *Rolling Stone Magazine* would later rank *Paul Simon* as number 266 on the list of the 500 Greatest Albums of All Time. The first hit to be released from the album was "Mother and Child Reunion."

Paul was interested in reggae, and the story goes that he was in a Chinese restaurant in New York City and saw that they had a menu item called "Mother and Child Reunion." He decided right then and there that this would be words in his next song. I have to stop here and say that there are some people who don't believe this story and that it is just an urban myth, but who knows, I've seen it in various places so I'd like to believe it.

The song is dedicated to a dog that Paul and Peggy Simon had a year or so earlier. The dog was struck by a car and killed and the Simons were still in mourning over the loss of the dog. "Mother and Child Reunion" has words which refer to this incident, and the song is very personal to Paul. Paul travelled to Jamaica and set up shop with the famous Jimmy Cliff's band, and they backed him on the song. It was released in February of 1972 and rose to number four on the Top 40 charts.

The next hit from the *Paul Simon* album was "Me and Julio Down By the Schoolyard." I can remember when I first heard that song and thinking I had never heard anything quite like it before, and I liked it. It was catchy, had a cool beat, and I felt Paul was as good as he ever was. The song is about two boys who commit some crime (we're not told what), "mama pajama" finds out and reports them to the police, but later they are released due to the efforts of a priest. All of this set to the infectious reggae rhythm. The song didn't do quite as well as the first hit, peaking at number twenty-two on the Top 40 charts.

ART GARFUNKEL ALONE

Art kept busy, too. He finished *Carnal Knowledge*, and the film was released. It drew mixed reviews. Some liked it and thought it taught a very important story. Others thought it was trash. Art was happy. He thought he had done a good job and was satisfied with the outcome. He had achieved what he had set out to do: be a movie star.

The movie was done and Art was now alone, professionally. He was still together with Linda Grossman, and there was talk of marriage, but it hadn't happened yet. Art knew that Paul was working on a solo album. Perhaps, he should do the same thing. This time, he would be in charge, and he would be the headliner.

But the album was slow in coming. Art wasn't a writer and had to select songs that others proposed to him. He had a lot of trouble making up his mind. It was not easy being number one.

There was a bright spot that happened in 1972. It was a presidential election year, and Richard Nixon was running against George McGovern. McGovern needed money for his campaign, and they decided to hold a fund raiser and invited both Paul and Art to sing together for the one night. Paul and Art both hated Nixon and said yes. It would be the first time they sang together for over two years, but it was not a reunion. They describe it as a one-shot thing that happened for one night and then the two went their own ways. There were still a lot of people who did not realize that they had split up.

In the summer of 1972, Clive Davis, the President of Columbia Records, did not want to believe that duo was done, so he released an album of their greatest hits. *Simon & Garfunkel's Greatest Hits* contained pretty much every hit they had had previously as a duo. However, unlike most greatest hits albums, four of the songs were live versions instead of the familiar versions. Proving Davis's theory that the public still loved the guys, the album peaked at number five in the United States and number four in England. I really like the picture on the cover of the album. I have always wanted a hat like Paul is wearing in the picture. That is probably my favorite picture of the two.

Art went back to working on his first solo album which was to be called *Angel Clare* and, I think, in an effort to be mysterious, Art named his album after the heroine in Thomas Hardy's book *Tess of the d'Urbervilles*. Art said he liked the sound of the words, *Angel Clare*.

In September of 1972, Peggy gave birth to Paul's first son, whom they named Harper (Peggy's maiden name). Art finally convinced Linda to marry him, and they tied the knot in October in Nashville. They had been together for four years. In what I consider a surprise, the Simons attended the wedding, and Paul and Art were very civil to each other. It appeared they were still friends; they just couldn't work together, anymore.

Angel Clare was going slowly. Columbia was a little worried but not much. Art was finding his own sound and his own identity. He could no longer depend on Paul for inspiration and, well, everything. So the album proceeded. It would finally be released in September of 1973. The album reached number five in the U.S., number six in Canada, and number fourteen in England, among other places. Columbia need not have worried; the album was a bona-fid hit.

Angel Clare produced two Top 40 songs, "All I Know" got to number nine; thus, hitting the Top 10 and "I Shall Sing" which peaked at number 38, just breaking into the Top 40. "All I Know" is, in my opinion, one of the greatest songs ever written. It is certainly my favorite Art Garfunkel song and gives me chills every time I hear it. It was written by the famous Jimmy Webb, one of America's greatest song writers. (Wow, "greatest" used twice in the same paragraph, that's how strongly I feel about this song.)

"THERE GOES RHYMIN' SIMON"

Meanwhile, Paul was hard at work on his second "post-group" solo album. *There Goes Rhymin' Simon* really shows the fun side of Paul Simon. Paul had a newborn son, and the child meant everything to him. Several of the songs on the new album are sung directly to Harper. Paul was really happy for the first time in a long time. He was experimenting with different styles of music, and the songs were coming fast. The album was finished in less than a year, which was a record (pun intended) for Paul. The album would do well in sales. It was released in May of 1973 and peaked at number two in the United States and number four in England.

Paul has various music styles on the album. He spent some time at Muscle Shoals in Alabama where he recorded about half of the album. He brought in the musicians who had played with the Staple Singers on "I'll Take You There," and they recorded with him on several tracks. He hired a Dixieland band from New Orleans to play behind him on "Take Me To the Mardi Gras" although you don't hear them until right near the end of the song. He asked The Dixie Hummingbirds, a gospel group, to sing with him on "Tenderness" and "Loves Me Like a Rock."

The most controversial song on the album has to be "Kodachrome. ®" The first line of the song includes the word "crap" which seems tame today, but this was the first time the word had been used in a major song. Some radio stations wouldn't play the song because they thought it was vulgar. To make matters worse, the word "Kodachrome" was a registered trademark and Eastman Kodak, who owed the trademark, insisted that the registered mark be on every album. Great Britain had a policy that it would not play or sell any record that purported to advertise a product, so "Kodachrome" was not even released in England.

When it came time to issue singles from the album, Paul wanted "American Tune" to be the first single. This is a lovely song, a ballad which is sung to his baby boy, Harper. He thought it could be another "Bridge Over Troubled Water." Columbia disagreed with that, and the record company ended up releasing "Kodachrome" as the first single. Despite all the controversy, the song reached number two on the American charts.

The second song from the album was "Loves Me Like a Rock" which also went to number two on the Billboard Top 40 charts and would spend fourteen weeks on the charts. This one was released in England where it peaked at number 39, probably because of the controversy of the first song.

The third and last single from the album was the song Paul wanted first, "American Tune," but even though this is a great song and a beautiful ballad, it only reached number thirty eight just making it into the Top 40. However, it was recognized for just how good it is. *Rolling Stone Magazine* voted it the Best Song of 1974.

A mention should be made of Paul's new producer, Phil Ramone. His former producer, who he still worked with occasionally, was Bill Halle, but Halle was on the West Coast and was busying working with Art, so Paul hired Ramone to do most of the *Rhymin' Simon* album. Ramone was already a famous producer, but he would go on to do many great things and work with people like Billy Joel and the band Chicago.

In late 1974, Art released a single, which was not attached to any album, called "Second Avenue" which hit the Top 40, peaking at number 34. He then got to work on his second solo album *Breakaway*.

PROBLEMS AT HOME

Even though Paul was happy with his career and with the music and loved that baby like nothing else, there was trouble brewing at home. Like many show business families, a lot of concessions have to be made when one member of the couple is gone a good deal of the time. Paul and Peggy had agreed that their marriage would be a 50-50 proposition, but Peggy was unhappy. She didn't think Paul was holding up his end of the partnership. How could he when he was gone on tour several months out of the year?

Sixteen months after the birth of Harper things finally came to a head, and Paul moved out. He went from happy to being depressed in an instant. It so happened that Art was having exactly the same kind of problems, and he and Linda decided to call it quits, also. Both men's lives were collapsing, and it was natural that they would gravitate toward each other. Art came to New York, and the two actually got together several times to talk and reminisce.

They tried to work together but too much time had passed, and it was difficult. In the spring of 1975, they were seen briefly together at the Grammy Awards. The Record of the Year that year was "I Honestly Love You" by Olivia Newton-John, and Paul and John Lennon came on stage to present the award. John made a joke about working with "Paul" again. It is a magical moment for someone like me who loves the music of these people. John Lennon announced the winner and who should come up to accept the award but Art Garfunkel himself. Olivia Newton-John was not there for some reason. They joked back and forth a little and Art said "Still writing, Paul?" Search for Grammys 1975 on YouTube and watch it, it's great.

Paul was hard at work on the next album *Still Crazy After All These Years*. I think for the post S&G era, this was his best work. The title song relates to him sitting in a hotel room staring out at the traffic right after he left Peggy and the despair he felt. Paul later said when the words came to him, he was in the shower and he just stood there and cried for twenty minutes. Money does not a happy life make.

The album was released in October, 1975 and reached number one on the Billboard album charts. This was his first album to hit number one since *Bridge*.

The single, which was the first released from the album, was the up tempo "Gone At Last" which features Phoebe Snow and the Jessy Dixon Singers. It has a distinct gospel sound. You can easily visualize the revival feeling of the song. Paul first recorded the song with Bette Midler but then decided he wanted a gospel sound to the song so the earlier version was scraped, and Phoebe Snow was asked to step in. She was thrilled. "Gone At Last" did chart, peaking at number twenty three on the Top 40.

It was the next song that would really do well, however, "50 Ways to Leave Your Lover" was released in December of 1975 and reached number one just about a month or so later on February 7th, 1976. This would be, so far, his only number one song as a solo artist, but it was a blockbuster, staying on the charts for thirteen weeks.

It is said that this song is about his breakup with Peggy. The number 50 was used because Peggy was always complaining that their marriage was not a 50-50 proposition. Paul was gone all of the time and didn't fulfill his half. Paul loved playing with little Harper and wanted the music to be fun and, even though the subject matter was serious, the tone of the song was catchy and lively and you can tell he is kind of making fun of the whole process.

"My Little Town"

In October of 1975, Paul hosted an episode of *Saturday Night Live* on NBC Television. In a surprise move that no one knew was coming, Art joined him on stage and they sang a couple of songs from the old days: "The Boxer" and "Scarborough Fair." Then they sang a new song that no one had heard before, "My Little Town." Paul had written the song just for Art's new album *Breakaway*, but Art felt it would sound better with harmony and that they should do it together.

Paul claims that the song is not biographical. It's mainly about a boy who is unhappy in his home town and wants out. Paul and Art never felt that way. Listen to the words. They are pretty depressing. Paul felt that the stuff Art was recording was too "sweet;" that he needed to shake things up a little, so, he wrote "My Little Town" for him. I think this shows that the two, while not really working together, were certainly on speaking terms and sincerely still liked each other.

Since there was no Simon & Garfunkel album to put the song on, and since both had sung on the song, they decided to put it on both albums. Thus, it is included both on Art's *Breakaway* and on Paul's *Still Crazy After All These Years*. The song was a big hit. This was the first time the duo had hit the charts since 1970. The song reached number nine on the Billboard Top 40.

The bit on *Saturday Night Live* was advertised as a Simon & Garfunkel reunion, but the guys didn't see it that way. To them, it was a one shot thing, and they really didn't intend to repeat it. Both Paul and Art later told the press that they were still friends but would probably never record together again as a duo. The occasional single, maybe, but not as a full time job.

The next single from the *Still Crazy* album was the title song, and I would have thought it would be a giant hit, but it struggled just to make the Top 40, peaking at number 40 and only staying on the charts for two weeks.

We have to back up a little to include Art in this discussion. He released *Breakaway* at almost exactly the same time Paul released *Still Crazy*, in October of 1975. He had already released the first single from the album which, for me, is his second greatest song. "I Only Have Eyes For You" is a beautiful song that you can slow dance to. It has quite a history. It was written way back in the Thirties. It was first, as far as I can tell, performed by the Ben Selvin Orchestra back in 1934 and was a number two song for him. Believe it or not, the song is on YouTube if you'd like to hear Selvin's version. It was a big hit in its day. Then an R&B group out of Chicago, The Flamingoes, recorded the song in a doo-wop style in 1959 and it peaked at number eleven on the charts. Art did not do quite that well, peaking at number eighteen, but there is no doubt in my mind that his version is the best. It did hit number one in England. They have such good taste.

Then "My Little Town" was released in late 1975 and, as I've said, reached number nine. After the release of the album *Breakaway* in October of 1975, Art released the title song and it just made the Top 40, peaking at number 39. Those would be the only three hits he had from the album, but singles do not necessarily make a successful album. *Breakaway* started out slow and only reached number nine on the album charts, but it continued to sell and was eventually pronounced platinum for the Recording Institute. It would become Art's biggest selling album of his solo career.

Both Paul and Art were now single, after their respective divorces had become final, they were both thirty-four years old, and it seemed that the world was their oyster, but neither was really happy. Paul did not feel like starting yet another album, and Art was gradually fading into the background. Could their careers be saved?

"Annie Hall"

Paul was good friends with movie director Woody Allen, and Allen was working on a new film starring Diane Keaton called *Annie Hall*. One day, he asked Paul if he'd like to have a small non-musical part in the movie. Paul, who had never gotten over the fact that Mike Nichols had cut him from his movie several years before, reluctantly agreed. During the filming of *Annie Hall*, Paul met a relatively new actress named Shelly Duval. The two hit it off right away. Duval was the type of person you could stay up all night talking to and never get tired. The two became lovers, and Duval moved in with Paul. This time, he actually did appear in the movie. He plays a man named Tony Lacey who is, amazingly, a rock star. Perfect casting.

In 1977, Jimmie Carter took over the White House and asked Paul to play for his inaugural ball. He sang "American Tune" which everyone thought was very appropriate for the occasion.

Art had also fallen in love again, also with an actress. Her name was Laurie Bird, and she was trying to break into pictures in a big way. In what I feel is a strange coincidence, Bird got a small role in the same picture Paul was working on, *Annie Hall*. It was her third and, unfortunately, her last picture. A year or so later, Bird killed herself while in Art's apartment in New York.

But before all of that, Art was slowly working on his next album *Watermark*. Columbia was impatient with the progress the album was making, so they released "Crying in My Sleep," a song from the album early to gauge public approval. The song tanked. It didn't even crack the Hot 100. Columbia panicked and decided what they needed was another "My Little Town." James Taylor had recently joined Columbia and so the producers joined him up with Paul and Art to form a trio and they recorded "What a Wonderful World." James and

Art blended together very well on the old Sam Cooke song. Sam Cooke had had a number twelve hit with the song back in 1960 and the newly formed trio made it to number eighteen with the song.

At about this same time, Columbia released the first *Paul Simon - Greatest Hits* album. It contained all of his solo hits and a couple of new songs. One, in particular, was Paul's next hit: "Slip Slidin' Away" which was Top 10, reaching number five. The background vocals for the song are done by the Oak Ridge Boys of Country music fame.

Life went on for both performers. Someone was always asking when they would get back together, but neither one was really interested in recording together again. Art released *Watermark* in October of 1977, but the only hit from the album was "Wonderful World." He followed that up with *Fate for Breakfast* in March of 1979, and it was his first album as a solo artist to miss the Top 40, peaking at number 67. He would never again break into the Top 40 (as of this writing). Both albums were well received by the critics, and *Watermark* could be considered a hit, but *Fate for Breakfast* did not sell well here, although it was a major hit in England reaching number two on their charts.

Fate for Breakfast does contain a song which I love. "Since I Don't Have You" is not quite as good as the original which was done by the group The Skyliners back in 1979. That is truly a rock and roll classic. They reached number twelve with the song, but Art only got to number 53, so he didn't break into the Top 40. A real shame, since it is a great song. This song has been done by many different singers and groups. No one, as yet, has equaled the Skyliners, in my opinion.

CARRIE FISHER

Paul spent the next couple years trying to write new music and appearing on *Saturday Night Live* on a regular basis. He had become friends with Lorne Michaels who was the producer of the show for many years. Shelly Duval got a movie role which took her to Europe and the two drifted apart. It was during his association with *Saturday Night Live* that he met Carrie Fisher.

Fisher, the daughter of Debbie Reynolds and Eddie Fisher, was a big star. She was in the middle of filming *Star Wars* when they met. She found she really liked Paul and soon the two were a pair who were constantly together. It was a weird pair up since Paul had sworn off all drugs many years before and Fisher was deep into the drug scene, taking everything she could get her hands on, but they seemed to get along fine.

Paul, having problems with Columbia, decided it was time to get out. He tried to get out of his contract and finally after two years of legal bickering, paid Columbia $1.5 million to release him and he was able to take his work with him. He then signed onto Warner Brothers Records so he could continue recording.

Also, Paul was at work on a screen play which would, in 1980, become the movie *One Trick Pony*. Paul insists the movie is not autobiographical, but it sounds to me a lot like Paul's life. The main character is a rock performer who is trying to put together a new album with a record company that won't support him. Also, his marriage is failing. When the movie was made, Paul played the leading role: a man named Jonah Levin.

Art had also become involved in a new movie which was filming in Europe. The movie, called *Bad Timing*, had an "X" rating several years ago when it was released. Now (2020), I notice they have downgraded it to an "R" rating. Laurie Rich, his live in girlfriend, was left alone in New York much of the time since Art was gone being an actor. Rich, already taking several drugs, upped the quantity as a result of being alone and on June 19th, 1980, she overdosed and died in Art's apartment.

The word was that Rich committed suicide, that it wasn't accidental. The main reason given was that Art would not commit to marriage, and she was despondent over that. No one will know for sure, but Laurie Rich was gone. Art, however, was devastated. He said he knew the exact moment she died; he could feel it. It took him six months before he really got over the death.

Both movies came out about the same time, 1980. *One Trick Pony* had the advantage of having a soundtrack which would sell separately. "Late in the Evening" was released from the album as a single and it reached number six on the charts. It would be Paul's last Top 10 song. The soundtrack did fairly well, peaking at number twelve on the album charts, but the movie not so much.

The critics, in large part, hated it. They called it one big advertisement for the album. They didn't think Paul was that good of an actor. Art was having exactly the same problem. *Bad Timing* was largely ignored by the public and several critics were not that impressed by his acting, either. Both went to their respective homes to lick their wounds and wonder what was next for the pair.

Neither man needed money. They were both rich beyond their wildest dreams. They had fame, money, everything anyone would want, but they weren't happy and neither could figure out why. The solution was just around the corner.

The Central Park Concert

One day in the summer of 1981, Paul got a call from New York City's concert liaison, Ron Delsener. He explained that several people had been doing concerts in Central Park for the purpose of revitalizing the park. James Taylor had done one. Elton John also had performed there. Would he be interested in getting together with Art and doing a reunion show? Paul thought it was a good idea. He saw it as a way to break out of the depression he was feeling about the movie and his career, in general.

Paul called Art, who was trying to shake off his own depression and asked if he'd liked to join him. Art was enthusiastic about the chance to sing and get together with Paul again. They had never stopped being friends, even after all these years.

There was a lot of talk about just how the concert should be done. Should the guys do solo acts and then join together and after much discussion, it was decided that they would do an entire Simon & Garfunkel concert, together for the entire time. For the solo songs, they would rehearse and do them together. But, of course, wonderful things do not come without some problems. There was some bickering about exactly what should be sung and whether to have a band or just the two of them with a guitar. On some songs, a piano was needed.

It was all worked out and on September 19th, 1981, the day had arrived. The day started out overcast, and they were afraid of rain, and it did rain off and on during the day, but it let up by concert time that evening. The people began to pour into Central Park. Thousands of them and then hundreds of thousands. At show time, it is estimated that there were over one-half million people in the park. This was one of the largest concerts ever held, even bigger than Woodstock. If you have seen pictures of the park during the concert, you can believe this.

The mayor of New York, Ed Koch, walked out on stage and just simply said, "Ladies and gentlemen, Simon and Garfunkel." The crowd went wild. The guys calmly walked out onto the stage and started the show. "Mrs. Robinson" was first, followed by "Homeward Bound" and then they were off. They sang Paul's solo numbers like "Me and Julio." Art sang right along like he had been doing them his whole life. Art sang a new song from his new album *Scissors Cut* called "A Heart in New York" and Paul sang right along with him.

It is said that the smell of marijuana was strong in the crowd. There were over 300 police officers on site in case of trouble, but there were virtually no arrests for drug possession.

You can watch the entire concert on YouTube. (Isn't everything on YouTube?) It runs one and a half hours long. In a tribute to their heroes, the Everly Brothers, they did "Wake Up Little Suzie," then for another hour, thrilled the crowd with every hit either of them had ever done, both together and separate. At one point, an over-zealous fan rushed the stage and had to be restrained by security, but it didn't bother the guys at all. They concluded the concert with "Sound of Silence" and left the stage. The crowd brought them back for an encore at which point they introduced the band and finished up with Paul's single "Late in the Evening." It was very dark in New York City by this time.

The next morning, there were still people camped out in the park. Bulldozers were brought in to clean up the mess and had to be careful not to run over sleeping bodies. It cost the city $20,000 just for cleanup. The reaction of Paul and Art was one of letdown. I think the high was so high during the concert, just the joy of having half a million people cheer for you, that nothing that came after could come close to it. They left the concert and went their separate ways. Would there be another concert like this? Probably not. Both Paul and Art went back to business as usual while America had one sensational evening.

But the public and the record companies would not let this be a one-shot deal. They convinced Paul and Art to do a reunion tour and so they did. They agreed with the provision that they wouldn't just do oldies but that the concerts would include new music as well. Everyone agreed. Unfortunately, it didn't work. All the old feelings came back, and it wasn't long before they were arguing about everything. They were expected to make an album together (Paul had already written the songs), but Art just wouldn't settle done and do the work. They both dragged their feet. The album was taking longer and longer and didn't look like it would ever be done.

Then the reunion tour began in Japan, and they had to work together. Sadly, relations grew worse and worse until they weren't even speaking to each other except when they were on stage. They got through the tour, but it was torture. Coming home, Paul wanted to finish his album, so he called Art and, in a terse statement, told him he was erasing all of Art's harmonies from the tracks. He was out of the album. The next week, he married Carrie Fisher.

They were married on August 16th, 1983 in a traditional Jewish wedding. Father Eddie Fisher gave the bride away. After going together for almost six years, you would think they could get along and knew each other pretty well but being married just did not work out. The marriage lasted only eleven months and the two spit up and were divorced.

When the reunion tour ended in Israel, it was billed as the "last Simon and Garfunkel concert ever." Paul, once again, had had enough and went home to finish his latest album, now called *Hearts and Bones*. The title song is a tribute to Carrie as their troubles hadn't really started yet. The album would only make number 35 on the Billboard Album chart. Two singles were released from the album, but neither one made the Top 40.

A song that deserves to be mentioned from the album was never a single or a hit but is an important song. It's called "The Late Great Johnny Ace." Paul sang it at the Central Park concert for the very first time in public and the song is about two "Johnnies:" one was Johnny Ace who was an R&B singer from 1955 who accidently killed himself playing Russian Roulette with a revolver. He had a big hit (at least at the time) with "Pledging My Love." If you haven't heard that lately or ever, check it out on YouTube, it's worth it. The other "Johnny" Paul is singing about is the late great John Lennon who was killed just a year or so before Paul wrote this song. Paul knew Lennon and the death was a great shock to him as it was to everyone.

Hearts and Bones would be a Paul Simon solo album since he had removed every bit of Art's contribution to the album. Paul felt this was the best work he had ever done and the critics agreed, but the public didn't see it that way. They wanted Simon & Garfunkel, not just one of them. Sales were slow and then died altogether. As I said, 35 was as high as it got. Paul was devastated. To make matters worse, his marriage to Carrie Fisher was falling apart less than a year after it started. Some say it was Carrie's drug use that killed it; others just blame it on incompatibility. I think Paul was going through so much heartache that it just leaked over into his marriage.

Art, too, was hurting. He hadn't gotten over the death of his girlfriend, Laurie Bird. He was dating again, this time Penny Marshall (of Laverne and Shirley fame) who he had met through Carrie Fisher, and they travelled a lot. Art's answer to problems was to travel. Get away and walk through some foreign country. He had done that a lot over the years, and he and Penny now left for Europe.

"Graceland"

When Paul was feeling bad, he would go off by himself and listen to music on the car radio. He happened to have a tape of music called *Gumboots: Accordion Jive Hits*. This was African music, and Paul got caught up in the rhythm and beats of the songs. You know the feeling: when you have been feeling bad for some reason and a certain song comes on the radio and all of a sudden your mood is lifted and you feel much better. This is what happened to Paul.

He determined to find out more about this music. In a way, it took him back to his roots, to the beginnings of rock and roll. He discovered that the music was called *mbaqanga* or "township jive." It started in South Africa in the early Sixties. In the Zulu language, the word means porridge. An entire television program was devoted to the creation of the *Graceland* album, but I will just give you an overview.

Paul decided to go to South Africa to hear the music first hand and perhaps record it for a new album. This was the mid-Eighties and apartheid was alive and well. The people who originated the music could not own the music. Paul had a reputation and used it to get into places where white men could not normally go. He hired some black musicians and just let them play. He didn't try to edit it or change it in any way. Some blacks did not want to work for Paul, thinking it would send the wrong message to the government. But enough did. Paul paid well and for two and half weeks, he recorded with several black bands in South Africa.

There was a cultural boycott of music from South Africa, and Paul generated a lot of criticism over working with black musicians. But, in the end, the good outvoted the bad. There are many well-known names on the album. The Everly Brothers sang with him on the title song "Graceland." Linda Ronstadt sang on "Under African Skies."

The group Los Lobos joined with Paul on the track "All Around the World or the Myth of Fingerprints," but when the album was released, Los Lobo was given no credit for the song. They claimed they had written the song and Paul had stolen it. It was all finally worked out and the album now shows co-writing credit on the song.

Four singles were released from *Graceland* but only one of them can be called a hit. The title song "Graceland" is said to not especially be about Elvis Presley's home but more about the innocence of early rock and roll. We go to "Graceland" when we go back and listen to the old stuff. The song only got to number 81 on the charts.

"You Can Call Me Al" was the only bona fide hit from the album and reached number twenty three on the Top 40. He has never hit the Top 40 again. If you were watching MTV in the Eighties, you might remember the video that was done for "You Can Call Me Al." It featured Paul and Chevy Chase, but Chase was doing the singing (or so it seemed as he lip synced to the song.) The two walk on stage and sit down in chairs while Chase is singing to the song and Paul stands up and walks out of the room to get instruments in the back room and just general foolishness ensues. I remember loving it when I first saw it; I just watched it again, and I still love it.

The *Graceland* album was Paul's best-selling album since *Bridge Over Troubled Water* peaking at number three on the album charts. It was number one in England and seven other countries. The album won the Grammy for Best Album of the Year in 1987 and the song "Graceland" won for Best Record of the Year in 1988.

IN THE YEARS SINCE

Paul continued to record and had several successful albums, but he never hit the singles charts again. *The Rhythm of the Saints* did very well in 1990 peaking at number four. He followed that with *Songs From the Capeman* in 1997 which went to number 42. Then there was *You're the One* (#19) in 2000, *Surprise* (#14) in 2006, and *So Beautiful So What* (#4) in 2011.

Art also continued to record, although not quite so much as Paul. He released *The Animals' Christmas* with Amy Grant in 1986, but it did not chart. Next was *Lefty* which peaked at number 134 in 1988. He followed that with *Songs From a Parent to a Child* (1997), *Everything Waits to Be Noticed* (2002), and *Some Enchanted Evening* (2007), none of which charted.

Art married Kathryn (Kim) Cermack in September of 1988, and they are still married to this day. They have two children: James and Beau Daniel Garfunkel.

On May 30th, 1992, Paul married Edie Brickell of Oak Cliff, Texas. They, also, are still married and have three children: sons Adrian Edward and Gabriel Elijah and daughter Lulu.

There is some dispute as to when Simon & Garfunkel actually ended. Some go back to the original breakup in 1970. Others say it was after the Concert at Central Park in 1981. After that concert, they went on a world-wide tour together, but things were never the same. The distance between them was just too much. Each had created his own career, and the pair just didn't mesh anymore. Paul said "Simon & Garfunkel only exists on stage, after the show, the entity Simon & Garfunkel does not exist anymore."

They briefly got together for 21 sold-out shows in New York in 1993. But nothing stuck.

They toured again in 2003 - 2004 called "The Old Friends Tour." I saw them during this tour when they came to Salt Lake City as I mentioned at the beginning of this work. They did it again in 2009. They get together occasionally and do benefits and short tours, but the team of Simon & Garfunkel is over. I really doubt if it will ever happen again. I think the problems are too deep to be reconciled. They can put their differences aside for a few hours and sing the old songs but doing new stuff and actually getting together to record will probably never happen again.

LEGACY OF SIMON & GARFUNKEL

In 1990, the duo was inducted into the Rock and Roll Hall of Fame. James Taylor gave the induction speech.

In 2007, PBS televised the *Gershwin Awards* (in honor of George and Ira Gershwin) which was an award given to a composer or performer for a lifetime of contribution to popular music. Paul Simon received the award that year. He was the first.

It is said that Simon & Garfunkel are the highest selling duo in rock and roll history.

They had won Grammy Awards in 1968 for Record of the Year and Best Contemporary Pop Performance - Vocal Duo Or Group (for "Mrs. Robinson) and Best Original Score Written for a Motion Picture or a Television Special (for *The Graduate*); in 1970 for Record of the Year, Album of the Year, Song of the Year, Best Arrangement Accompanying Vocalist(s), Best Engineered Recording - Non-Classical, and Best Contemporary Song (all for *Bridge Over Troubled Water.*)

In 2003, they received the Lifetime Achievement Grammy Award, the highest award the Grammys gives out.

Between 1983 and 1997, Art Garfunkel literally walked across America. He did it in 40 separate pieces with breaks between. That's why it took fourteen years.

Paul received Kennedy Center Honors in 2002 from President George Bush. Paul McCartney was scheduled to receive it but had a conflict and couldn't attend, so Paul was honored.

Paul was inducted into the Rock and Roll Hall of Fame as a solo artist in 2002. He was inducted by Marc Anthony.

James Hoag

It is estimated that Simon & Garfunkel have sold over 100 million albums worldwide. They have sold 38 million in the United States alone.

Graceland alone sold over 14 million copies for Paul.

AFTERWORD

Simon & Garfunkel only released five original albums as a duo. Everything else was either a live album or a greatest hits album. Yet, who would dispute that the Simon & Garfunkel sound was the sound of the Sixties?

They came on the scene at precisely the right time. It can be argued that some luck had to do with their fame, but nobody can deny the talent that was Paul Simon and Art Garfunkel. Paul is one of the writing greats of our generation. His work has and will continue to stand the test of time. Art has one of the best voices to come along in the Twentieth Century. They complimented each other perfectly. It's too bad that they couldn't get along.

I write these books as much for myself as I do for the reader. It gives me a chance to go back and listen to all of the music. I grew up listening to this music and writing these short biographies takes me back to a simpler and (sometimes) a more innocent time. There's really not much that is innocent about Simon & Garfunkel but compared to today's music, they told stories that remind us of our childhood and make us feel good.

You can contact me at http://www.number1project.com where I occasionally blog about things that interest me in the music world (mostly, the twentieth century). Go find it and read it and leave me a comment. I also have a Facebook fan page called "Legends of Rock & Roll". "Like" me and comment there, too. If you love the music as much as I do, you'll enjoy the trip. Thanks for reading.

I hope you have enjoyed this book as much as I have enjoyed writing it for you.

James Hoag

If you have liked what you read, will you please do me a favor and leave a review of "Simon & Garfunkel". Thank you.

About the Author

James Hoag has always been a big fan of Rock & Roll. Most people graduate from high school and then proceed to "grow up" and go on to more adult types of music. James got stuck at about age 18 and has been an avid fan of popular music ever since. His favorite music is from the Fifties, the origin of Rock & Roll and which was the era in which James grew up. But he likes almost all types of popular music including country music.

After working his entire life as a computer programmer, he is now retired, and he decided to share his love of the music and of the performers by writing books that discuss the life and music of the various people who have meant so much to him over the years.

He calls each book a "love letter" to the stars that have enriched our lives so much. These people are truly Legends.

Selected Discography

Simon & Garfunkel Together

Studio Albums

1964 - Wednesday Morning, 3 A.M.

1966 - Sounds of Silence

1966 - Parsley, Sage, Rosemary and Thyme

1968 - Bookends

1970 - Bridge Over Troubled Water

Live albums

1982 - The Concert in Central Park

2002 - Live from New York City, 1967

2004 - Old Friends: Live on Stage

2008 - Live 1969

Soundtracks

1968 - The Graduate

Singles

1957 - "Hey Schoolgirl" (as Tom & Jerry)

1958 - "Our Song" (as Tom & Jerry)

1958 - "That's My Story" (as Tom & Jerry)

1959 - "Baby Talk"

Legends of Rock & Roll – Simon & Garfunkel

1962 - "Surrender, Please Surrender"

1963 - "I'm Lonesome"

1965 - "The Sound of Silence"

1966 - "Homeward Bound"

1966 - "That's My Story" [re-release]

1966 - "I Am a Rock"

1966 - "The Dangling Conversation"

1966 - "A Hazy Shade of Winter"

1967 - "At the Zoo"

1967 - "Fakin' It"

1968 - "Scarborough Fair/Canticle"

1968 - "Mrs. Robinson"

1969 - "The Boxer"

1970 - "Bridge over Troubled Water"

1970 - "Cecilia"

1970 - "El Condor Pasa (If I Could)"

1972 - "America"

1972 - "For Emily, Whenever I May Find Her" (live)

1975 - "My Little Town"

1982 - "Wake Up Little Susie"

1991 - "A Hazy Shade of Winter"/"Seven O'Clock News/Silent Night"

1992 - "The Boxer" [re-release]

Paul Simon Solo

Studio Albums

1965 - The Paul Simon Songbook (not released in the US until 2004)

1972 - Paul Simon

1973 - There Goes Rhymin' Simon

1975 - Still Crazy After All These Years

1983 - Hearts and Bones

1986 - Graceland

1990 - The Rhythm of the Saints

1997 - Songs from The Capeman

2000 - You're the One

2006 - Surprise

2011 - So Beautiful or So What

Soundtracks

1980 - One-Trick Pony

Live albums

1974 - Paul Simon in Concert: Live Rhymin'

1991 - Paul Simon's Concert in the Park, August 15, 1991

2012 - Live In New York City

Singles

1958 - "True or False"/"Teenage Fool" (as True Taylor)

1959 - "Anna Belle"/"Loneliness" (as Jerry Landis)

1959 - "Don't Take the Stars"/"So Tenderly" (as a member of The Mystics)

1960 - "Just a Boy"/"Shy" (as Jerry Landis)

1960 - "Just a Boy"/"I'd Like to Be" (as Jerry Landis)

1960 - "All Through the Night"/"(I Begin) To Think Again of You" (as a member of The Mystics)

1960 - "Swanee"/"Toot, Toot, Tootsie, Goodbye" (as Jerry Landis)

1961 - "I Wish I Weren't in Love"/"I'm Lonely" (as Jerry Landis)

1961 - "Play Me A Sad Song"/"It Means a Lot to Them" (as Jerry Landis)

1961 - "Motorcycle"/"I Don't Believe Them" (as a member of Tico & The Triumphs)

1962 - "Express Train"/"Wildflower" (as a member of Tico & The Triumphs)

1962 - "Cry, Little Boy, Cry"/"Get Up And Do The Wobble" (as a member of Tico & The Triumphs)

1962 - "The Lone Teen Ranger"/"Lisa" (as Jerry Landis)

1962 - "Cards of Love"/"Noise" (as a member of Tico & The Triumphs)

1965 - "I Am a Rock"/"Leaves That Are Green"

1972 - "Mother and Child Reunion"/"Paranoia Blues"

1972 - "Me and Julio Down by the Schoolyard"/"Congratulations"

James Hoag

1972 - "Duncan"/"Run That Body Down"

1973 - "Kodachrome"/"Tenderness"

1973 - "Loves Me Like a Rock"/"Learn How to Fall"

1973 - "American Tune"/"One Man's Ceiling is Another Man's Floor"

1973 - "Take Me to the Mardi Gras"/"Something So Right"

1973 - "Something So Right"

1973 - "St. Judy's Comet"

1974 - "The Sound of Silence"/"Mother and Child Reunion"

1975 - "Gone at Last" (with Phoebe Snow and The Jessy Dixon Singers)/"Tenderness"

1975 - "50 Ways to Leave Your Lover"/"Some Folks' Lives Roll Easy"

1976 - "Still Crazy After All These Years"/"I Do It for Your Love"

1976 - "Have a Good Time"

1977 - "Slip Slidin' Away"/"Something So Right"

1978 - "Wonderful World" (with Art Garfunkel and James Taylor)/"Wooden Planes"(Art Garfunkel solo)

1978 - "Stranded in a Limousine"/"Have a Good Time"

1980 - "Late in the Evening"/"How the Heart Approaches What It Yearns"

1980 - "One-Trick Pony"/"Long, Long Day"

1981 - "Oh, Marion"/"God Bless the Absentee"

1983 - "The Blues" (with Randy Newman)/ "Same Girl" (Randy Newman solo)

1983 - "Allergies"/"Think Too Much"

1984 - "Think Too Much"/"Song About the Moon"

1986 - "You Can Call Me Al"/"Gumboots"

1986 - "Graceland"/"Hearts and Bones"

1987 - "The Boy in the Bubble"/"Crazy Love, Vol. II"

1987 - "Diamonds on the Soles of Her Shoes"/"All Around the World, or the Myth of Fingerprints"

1990 - "The Obvious Child"

1990 - "Proof"

1990 - "Born at the Right Time"

1991 - "Still Crazy After All These Years" (live)

1995 - "Something So Right" (with Annie Lennox)

2000 - "Old"

2000 - "You're the One"

2003 - "Father and Daughter"

2006 - "Father and Daughter"

2006 - "That's Me"

2006 - "Outrageous"

2010 - "Getting Ready for Christmas Day"

2011 - "The Afterlife"

2012 - "The Boxer" (with Jerry Douglas feat. Mumford & Sons)

Art Garfunkel Solo

Studio albums

1973 - Angel Clare

1975 - Breakaway

1977 - Watermark

1979 - Fate for Breakfast

1981 - Scissors Cut

1986 - The Animals' Christmas (with Amy Grant)

1988 - Lefty

1997 - Songs from a Parent to a Child

2002 - Everything Waits to Be Noticed (with Maia Sharp and Buddy Mondlock)

2007 - Some Enchanted Evening

Live albums

1996 - Across America

Soundtracks

1978 – Watership Down, "Bright Eyes"

1989 – Sing, "We'll Never Say Goodbye"

1992 – A League Of Their Own, "Two Sleepy People"

1998 – As Good As It Gets, "Always Look On The Bright Side Of Life"

Legends of Rock & Roll – Simon & Garfunkel

1998 – Arthur and Friends: The First Almost Real Not Live CD (or Tape), "The Ballad of Buster Baxter"

Singles

1959 - "Beat Love"/"Dream Alone" (as Artie Garr)

1961 - "Forgive Me"/"Private World"

1973 - "All I Know"/"Mary Was an Only Child"

1973 - "I Shall Sing"/"Feuilles-Oh: Do Space Men Pass Dead Souls on Their Way to the Moon?"

1974 - "Travelling Boy"/"Old Man"

1974 - "Second Avenue"/"Woyaya"

1975 - "Breakaway"/"Disney Girls"

1975 - "I Only Have Eyes for You"/"Looking For the Right One"

1975 - "My Little Town" (With Paul Simon)/"Rag Doll"

1975 - "I Believe When I Fall In Love"/"Same Old Tears On A New Background"

1976 - "Woyaya"/"Down in the Willow Garden"

1977 - "Crying In My Sleep"/"Mr. Shuck 'N' Jive"

1978 - "Wonderful World" (With Paul Simon and James Taylor)/"Wooden Panes"

1978 - "Marionette"/"Someone Else"

1979 - "In A Little While (I'll Be On My Way)"/"And I Know"

1979 - "Since I Don't Have You"/"When Someone Doesn't Want You"

James Hoag

1979 - "Bright Eyes"/"When Someone Doesn't Want You"

1981 - "A Heart In New York"/"Is This Love"

1981 - "Scissors Cut"/"In Cars"

1981 - "Hang On In"/"Up in the World"

1981 - "The Romance"/"Bright Eyes"

1984 - "Sometimes When I'm Dreaming"/"The Decree"

1986 - "The Decree"/"Carol of The Birds" (with Amy Grant)

1988 - "When a Man Loves a Woman"/"I Have A Love"

1988 - "This Is The Moment"/"Slow Breakup"

1988 - "So Much In Love"/"King Of Tonga"

1994 - "Crying in the Rain" (With James Taylor)

1996 - "Grateful (Live)"/"I Will"

1997 - "Daydream"

2002 - "Bounce"

Printed in Great Britain
by Amazon